CHUCKLES AND SMILES

CHILDREN'S POEMS

WRITTEN BY
RAVEN HOWELL

ILLUSTRATED BY
JORDAN WRAY

ISBN: 978-1-7350915-5-6 (hard cover)
          978-1-7350915-6-3 (soft cover)
Editing: Amy Ashby

Published by Warren Publishing
Charlotte, NC
www.warrenpublishing.net
Printed in the United States

When I was asked to write a children's book for the simple intent of eliciting a giggle or a grin, I knew I wanted my words to sing to your heart and convey the joyful dance of sharing happiness with one another.

This is for your smile and inner light.
—Raven

CONTENTS

HYENAS

Are hysterical,
they **HEE** and **HAW** and **HOOT**.
You'd think that owls would do such things,
but they don't give a toot!

A TREE

A tree will gift you birds and shade,
a fluttering **COLOR** parade.
A tree will lift you on its shoulder
where the sky is **BIGGER**, bolder.

WIND

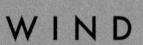

It made a silly, whistling noise
when I went to bed.
Today it SWUNG the birdhouse,
the one we painted red.
It brushes out my long hair,
tickling my neck.
Can't see the wind except for how
it BLOWS a snowflake speck.

SOCK PUPPET

This puppet has a GOOFY grin,
his pointy nose a silver pin.
Cute, winking eyes,
two glued on rocks,
it's STINKY though,
my brother's sock!

9

SPAGHETTI

Pasta noodles from the pot,
cold sesame or saucy HOT.

Twirled on forks, tied up in knots—
they end up in my lap
A LOT!

BABY LETTUCE

Baby lettuce feels grown up,
doesn't want a sippy cup.
Do not baby lettuce or it becomes a garden menace,
crying soggy baby tears for all Bibb lettuces to hear.
Then curls up in a muddy dress,
ending in a wilted

MESS!

WHO WOULD HAVE THOUGHT?

Campers always bring an axe
to CHOP the wood and pile up stacks.

A carpenter has cans and pails
of screws and nuts and nails.

A cook will use a knife and spoon
to STIR the pot or pit the prune.

For me,
In days spent at our school,
my BRAIN, it seems, is my best tool!

THE PIZZA POEM

The word "pizzazz" reminds me of pizza,
with two "ZZs," an "A," and cheese to feast on.
Adding pizzazz means to do it with flair,
so bake mine with lots of anchovies to spare!

THUD AND SPLASH

Raindrops on umbrellas **THUD,**
Piggy's playing in the **MUD!**

SQUIRREL

Bulb digger,
nest rigger,
seed stacker,
nut cracker,
tree stalker,
fence walker,
food stasher,
birdhouse crasher.
Dog chased—
making *HASTE*! 15

PICKLED

Johnny the joker got into a PICKLE.
Now he sits in a jar, a dill for a NICKEL.

BAREFOOT

Today the sun shines yellow,
the sky blends streaky blues.
It's getting warmer out now
and I don't wear my shoes.
Clover caught between my toes
brings HAPPY summer news.
The grass is good at tickling me
when I don't wear my SHOES!

17

MUSHROOM NAPS

Mushrooms wear those **SPONGY** caps
for little shaded buggy naps.

HATS

A sun visor for summer wear,
baseball caps in autumn air.
A WOOL hat wards off winter's sneezes,
rain hoods shield spring's drizzled breezes.
Bright hats fly in WINDY skies,
top hats hide rabbits inside.
Cats in hats sleep snug in beds,
but most hats are on top of heads!

19

MARCH

March comes in on tippy-toes,
nudging us from winter's doze.
Puckers up its CHILLY lips,
blowing us a kiss that nips.
It keeps its secrets—we don't know ...
we wait for either—SUN or SNOW!

20

PETE, MY DINO

Pete, my Dino, loves to bake
cookies, pies, and chocolate cake.
Whisks and bowls, and top chef hat ...
the taste testers? ME and my CAT!

SEED

Tiny seed,
in it goes.
Pat the soil,
let it DOZE.
Springtime comes, seed wakes up,
yellow as a BUTTERCUP!

A CREEPY REQUEST

Witches, goblins, little ghosts,
you zombies, and *UNDEAD*:
stay tucked on pages in my book,
don't creep under my *BED*!

23

UGH! BUG!

Bug, you're quicker than a WINK,
sometimes I wonder what you think.
Don't want to let this day go south,
so why fly straight into my MOUTH?

AROUND A BALLOON

Don't say poke,
don't say jab,
don't say POP
or pin or stab.
You might not want to mention prick,
and never speak of hole or nick.
Offer words
that lift and fly,
like float and waft,
or DRIFT and sky.

PUDDLE PLACE

Same hair, same face,
but in a   puddle place.
Just like me, holds my toy,
the water   a puddle boy.

26

SNAKE-Y SNAKE

My snake-y snake
will make-y make
an "S" shape just for fun.
He'll SHAKE-Y shake
then bake-y bake,
under the summer SUN.

27

BEE

Buzzing

Energetic

Equipped with stingers

LOOK WHAT HAPPENS!

Rain clouds slip from stormy skies,
RAINBOWS bound in by surprise!

29

BUTTERFLIES

If thunder **ROLLS**
and clouds fill skies,
it helps to **DREAM** of
butterflies.

TICKLES

Remember if today is crummy
you'll find a tickle in your TUMMY.
A warm and sunny kind of chummy
that wants to burst from head to BUMMY!

31

AUTHOR

Raven Howell is an award-winning picture book author. She writes poetry for a variety of children's magazines such as *Cricket* and *Highlights*, and enjoys visiting students in schools and libraries.

Raven is happiest on dawn hikes, at the seashore, being with her family, and in the inspiration of every day.

ILLUSTRATOR

Jordan Wray is an international children's author and illustrator. With crayons as fingers, Jordan has always loved to draw and is inspired by the world around him, especially his little black cat, Iver.

When he isn't writing or illustrating, Jordan spends most of his time caring for his house plants and dreaming about one day visiting the moon!

CPSIA information can be obtained
at www.ICGtesting.com
Printed in the USA
BVHW021756150820
586528BV00004B/101